Find & Speak
Welsh Words

Louise Millar and Llinos Dafydd

Illustrations by Louise Comfort

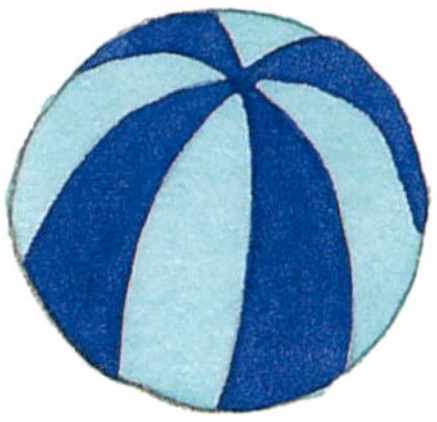

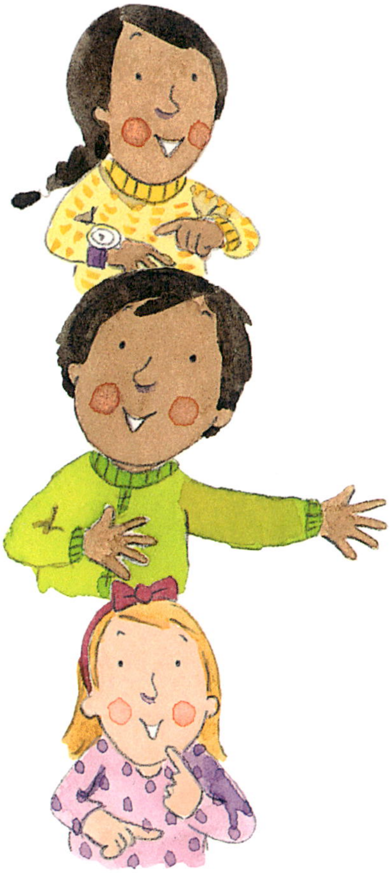

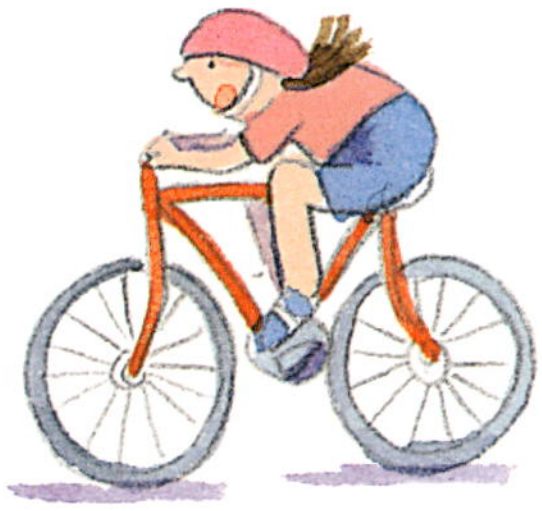

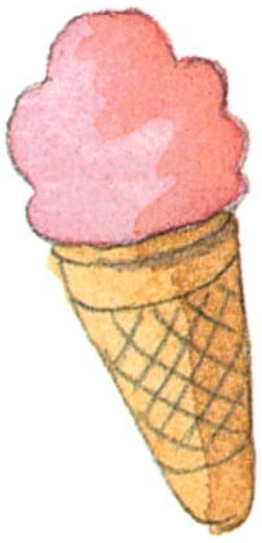

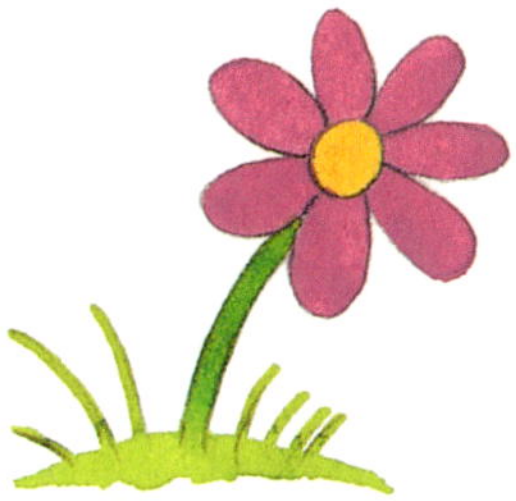

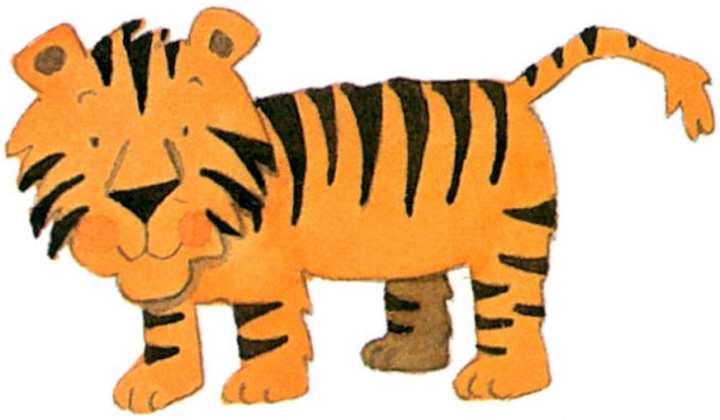

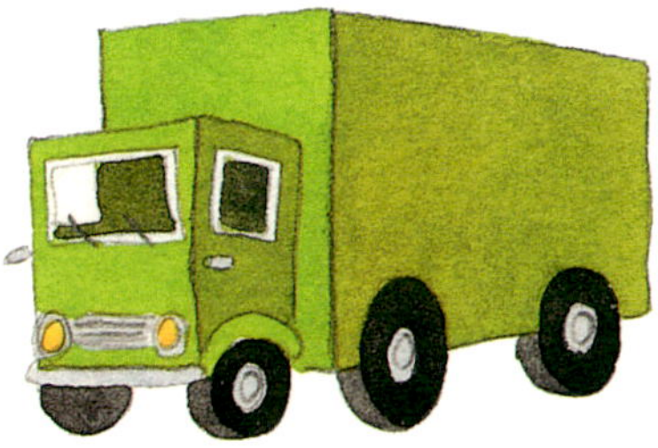

www.rily.co.uk

Ar y fferm

Look for these words in the big picture.

ceffyl
<u>keh</u>-fil
horse

buwch
* boowch
cow

ci
<u>key</u>
dog

Can you find another cat somewhere in the book?

llygoden fawr
* llchuh-go-den
rat

On the farm

mochyn
mohch-in
pig

dafad
* dah-vad
sheep

hwyaden
* hoowee-ah-den
duck

gafr
*gahvr
goat

cath
* kath
cat

Say the Welsh word aloud.

Yn y dosbarth

Look for these words in the big picture.

athro
ah-throah
teacher

cadair
* kah-dah-ire
chair

bwrdd
boowrth
table

pensil lliw
pen-sill llioow
coloured pencil

Find another chair somewhere in the book.

4

In the classroom

llyfr
llchuh-vir
book

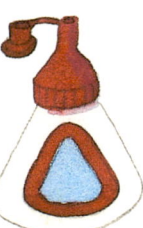

glud
gleed
glue

cyfrifiadur
kuh-vriv-yah-dir
computer

pen
pen
pen

papur
pap-ihr
paper

Say the Welsh word aloud.

5

Dy gorff

pen
pen
head

llygaid
** lluh-guide
eyes

trwyn
trooween
nose

ceg
* kehg
mouth

Your body

llaw

* llchaoow

hand

coes

* koyss

leg

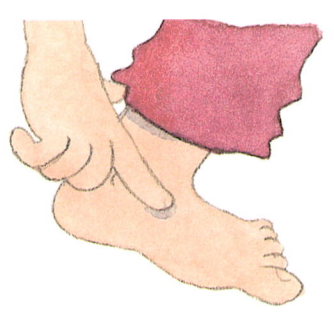

troed

* troid

foot

ysgwyddau

us-goowee-th-eye

shoulders

Say the Welsh word aloud.

braich

* brah-ike-ch

arm

Lliwiau yn y jyngl

Look for these words in the big picture.

coch
kohch
red

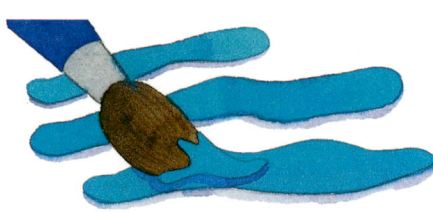

glas
glass
blue

How many purple things are in the scene?

gwyrdd
goow-erth
green

melyn
meh-lin
yellow

Colours in the jungle

gwyn
gwin
white

porffor
<u>pohr</u>-for
purple

brown
brohoown
brown

oren
<u>ohr</u>-ehn
orange

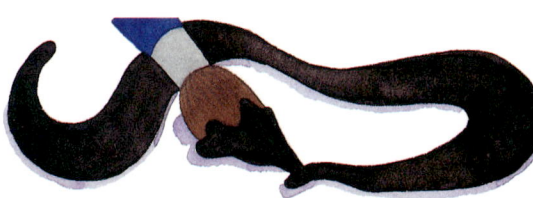

du
dee
black

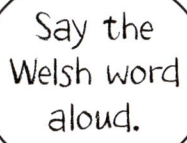

Say the Welsh word aloud.

Y bocs gwisgoedd ffansi

Look for these words in the big picture.

sgert
* sghert
skirt

ffrog
* frog
dress

Find someone on another page wearing a hat.

esgidiau
eh-skid-ee-eye
shoes

Say the Welsh word aloud.

The dressing-up box

trowsus
troh-oowsis
trousers

crys
crease
shirt

cot
* cot
coat

sanau
san-eye
socks

het
* het
hat

pyjamas
pyjamas
pyjamas

Yn y sw

Look for these words in the big picture.

jiráff
giraffe
giraffe

llew
llche-oow
lion

teigr
tay-gerr
tiger

crocodeil
crocodile
crocodile

Find another animal in the book that could be in the zoo.

At the zoo

eliffant
elephant
elephant

arth wen
* ahrth oowen
polar bear

hipo
hippo
hippopotamus

neidr
* <u>nay</u>-derr
snake

Say the Welsh word aloud.

dolffin
dolphin
dolphin

Pethau sy'n symud

Look for these words in the big picture.

bws
boows
bus

arhosfan bws
** ar-<u>hos</u>-van boows
bus stop

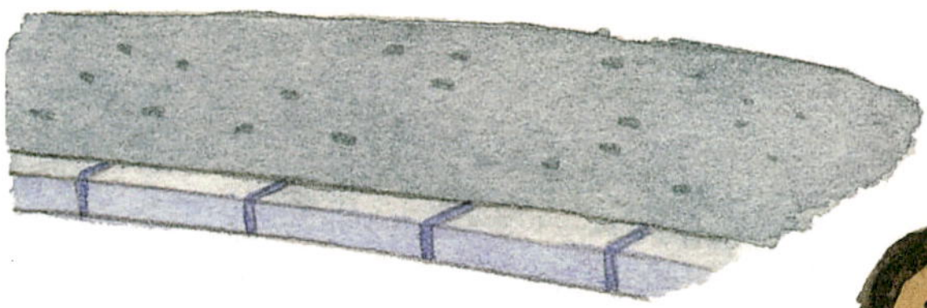

palmant
<u>pahl</u>-mant
pavement

Find a car somewhere else in the book.

stryd
* streed
street

Things that go

goleuadau traffig
goh-ley-<u>ahd</u>-eye <u>trah</u>fig
traffic lights

beic
bike
bicycle

car
car
car

lorri
* <u>loh</u>ree
lorry

Say the Welsh word aloud.

car heddlu
car <u>heth</u>lee
police car

Ar y traeth

Look for these words in the big picture.

gwylan
* <u>goowee</u>-lan
seagull

pysgodyn
pus-<u>gohd</u>-in
fish

cragen
* <u>krah</u>-gehn
shell

môr
m<u>o</u>re
sea

Find a fish on another page.

At the beach

gwymon
goowee-mohn
seaweed

craig
* cr-eye-g
rock

cwch hwylio
coowch hooweel-ee-oh
sailing boat

tywod
tow-od
sand

Say the Welsh word aloud.

ton
* ton
wave

Fy nheulu

Look for these words in the big picture.

brawd
broud
brother

chwaer
* chwa-ire
sister

tad
tahd
father

mam
* mam
mother

How many people are in your family?

My family

ewythr
eoow-ee-ther
uncle

modryb
* moh-dribb
aunt

mam-gu / nain
* mam-ghee / nine
grandmother

cefndryd
keven-drid
cousins

tad-cu / taid
tad-kee / taeed
grandfather

Say the Welsh word aloud.

Amser parti!

Look for these words in the big picture.

brechdan
* breh-ch-dan
sandwich

hufen iâ
hee-ven yah
ice cream

cacen / teisen
* kak-en / * tay-sen
cake

sglodion
sklod-dee-on
chips

Find some some balloons in another scene.

20

Party time!

diod swigod

* <u>dee</u>-od swig-od
fizzy drink

sudd oren

seethe <u>ohr</u>-ehn
orange juice

dŵr

d-<u>oow</u>-r
water

pitsa

pizza
pizza

siocled

<u>shock</u>-led
chocolate

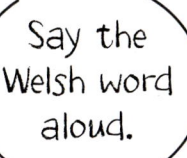

Say the Welsh word aloud.

Siopa am deganau

Look for these words in the big picture.

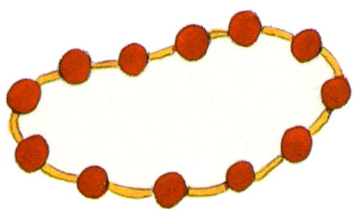

gleiniau
glayn-ee-eye
beads

robot
robot
robot

jig-so
jigsaw
puzzle

Find a teddy bear in another scene.

pêl-droed bwrdd
pehl-droid boowrth
table football

Shopping for toys

pêl
* pehl
ball

gêm
* gehm
game

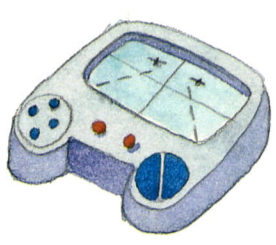

gêm gyfrifiadur
* gehm guh-vriv-yah-dihr
computer game

Say the Welsh word aloud.

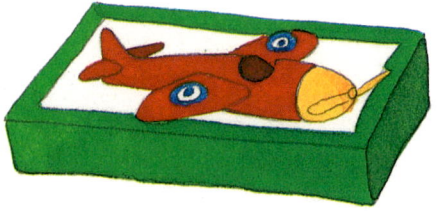

cit awyren fodel
kit ah-oow-uhr-ehn vodelle
model aeroplane kit

tedi
teddy
teddy

Yn y gegin

Look for these words in the big picture.

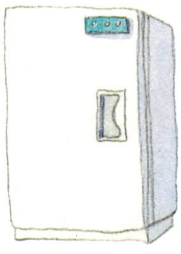

oergell
* <u>oi</u>-<u>err</u>-gehl-llch
fridge

gwydr
<u>goow</u>-<u>ee</u>-dr
glass

sosban
* <u>sos</u>-ban
saucepan

Find a glass on another page.

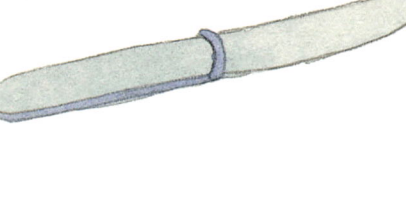

cyllell
* <u>kuh</u>-llcheh-llch
knife

In the kitchen

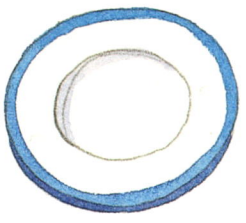

plat
plaht
plate

popty
pop-tee
cooker

sinc
* sink
sink

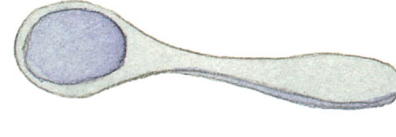

llwy
* llchoow<u>oi</u>
spoon

fforc
* foh-rk
fork

Say the Welsh word aloud.

Yng nghefn gwlad

Look for these words in the big picture.

coeden
* <u>coy</u>-den
tree

blodyn
<u>bloh</u>-din
flower

Find another bird in the book.

cae
ka-ee
field

coedwig
* <u>kohyd</u>-oowig
forest

In the country

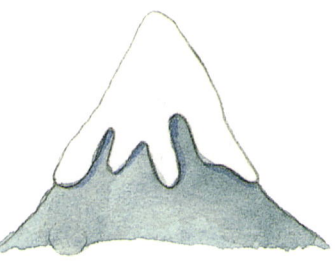

mynydd
muhn-ith
mountain

porfa
* pohr-va
grass

aderyn
ah-dehr-in
bird

pont
* pont
bridge

Say the Welsh word aloud.

afon
* ahvon
river

Cael bath

Look for these words in the big picture.

sebon
<u>seh</u>-bon
soap

basn ymolchi
basn uh-<u>mohl</u>-khee
washbasin

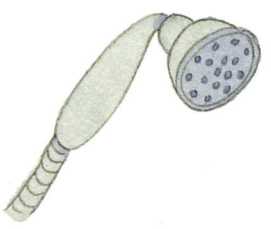

cawod
* <u>kahoow</u>-ohd
shower

tywel
tuhoow-ehl
towel

Find a bathroom on another page in the book.

Having a bath

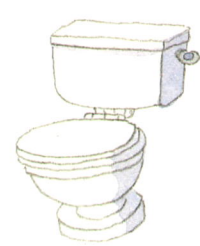

tŷ bach
tee bach
toilet

drych
dreech
mirror

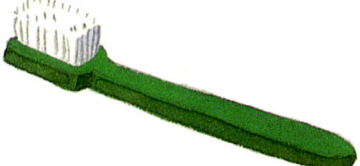

brwsh dannedd
broowsh dan-eth
toothbrush

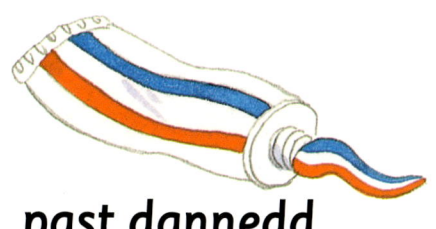

past dannedd
pahst dan-eth
toothpaste

Say the Welsh word aloud.

bath
bath
bath

Yn fy ystafell wely

Look for these words in the big picture.

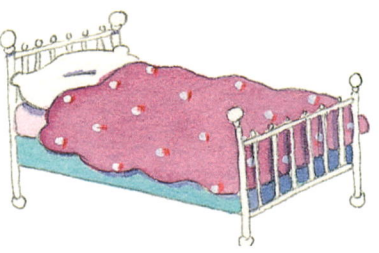

gwely
goow-<u>eh</u>-lee
bed

cwpwrdd dillad
<u>coop</u>-oorth <u>dee</u>-llchad
wardrobe

silff
* silf
shelf

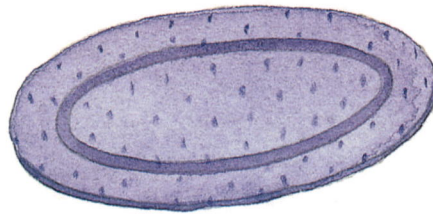

ryg
rug
rug

Find a bed in another picture in the book.

30

In my bedroom

teledu
tel-<u>eh</u>-dee
television

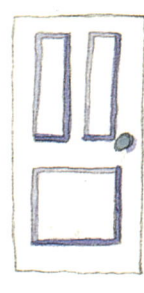

ffenest
* <u>feh</u>-nest
window

drws
droowss
door

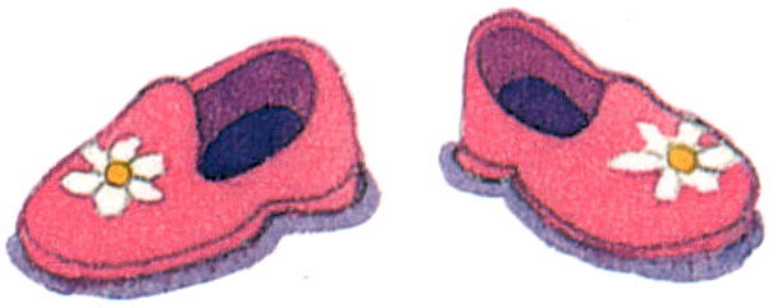

sliperi
slip-<u>air</u>-ee
slippers

cloc larwm
clock <u>lah</u>roowm
alarm clock

Say the Welsh word aloud.

Fy nhŷ

Look for these words in the big picture.

toiled
<u>toil</u>-<u>ed</u>
toilet

ystafell ymolchi
* uh-<u>stah</u>-vell uh-<u>mohl</u>-key
bathroom

nenfwd
* <u>nen</u>-vood
ceiling

y gegin
* uh <u>geh</u>-gihn
kitchen

Find another house in the book.

My house

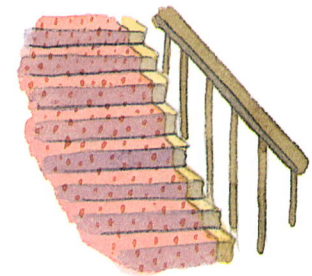

grisiau
grees-ee-eye
stairs

gardd
* gare-th
garden

to
toh
roof

lolfa
* lohl-va
sitting room

Say the Welsh word aloud.

ystafell wely
* uh-stah-vell ooweh-lee
bedroom

Yn ystod yr wythnos

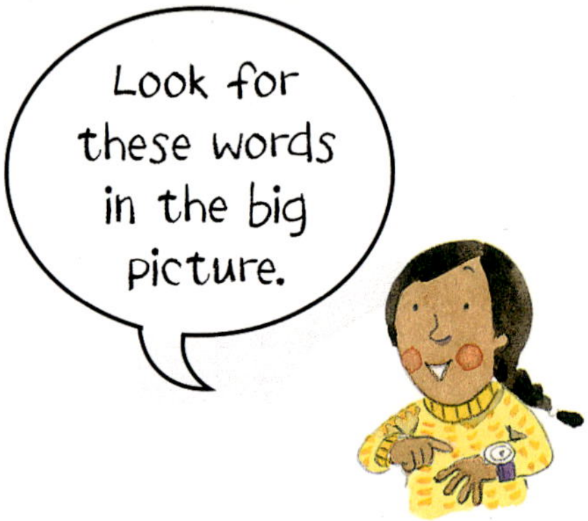

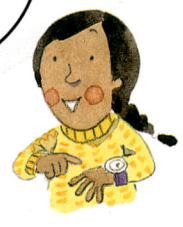

Look for these words in the big picture.

1
2
3
4
5
6
7

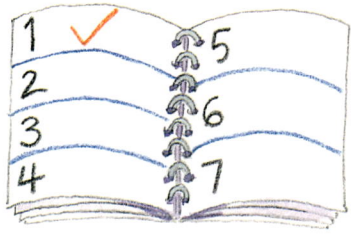

Dydd Llun

deeth llch-een

Monday

1
2
3
4
5
6
7

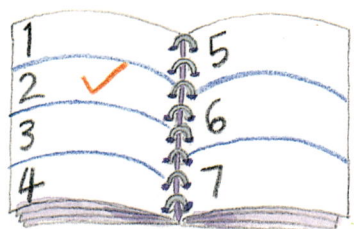

Dydd Mawrth

deeth mah-oorth

Tuesday

1
2
3
4
5
6
7

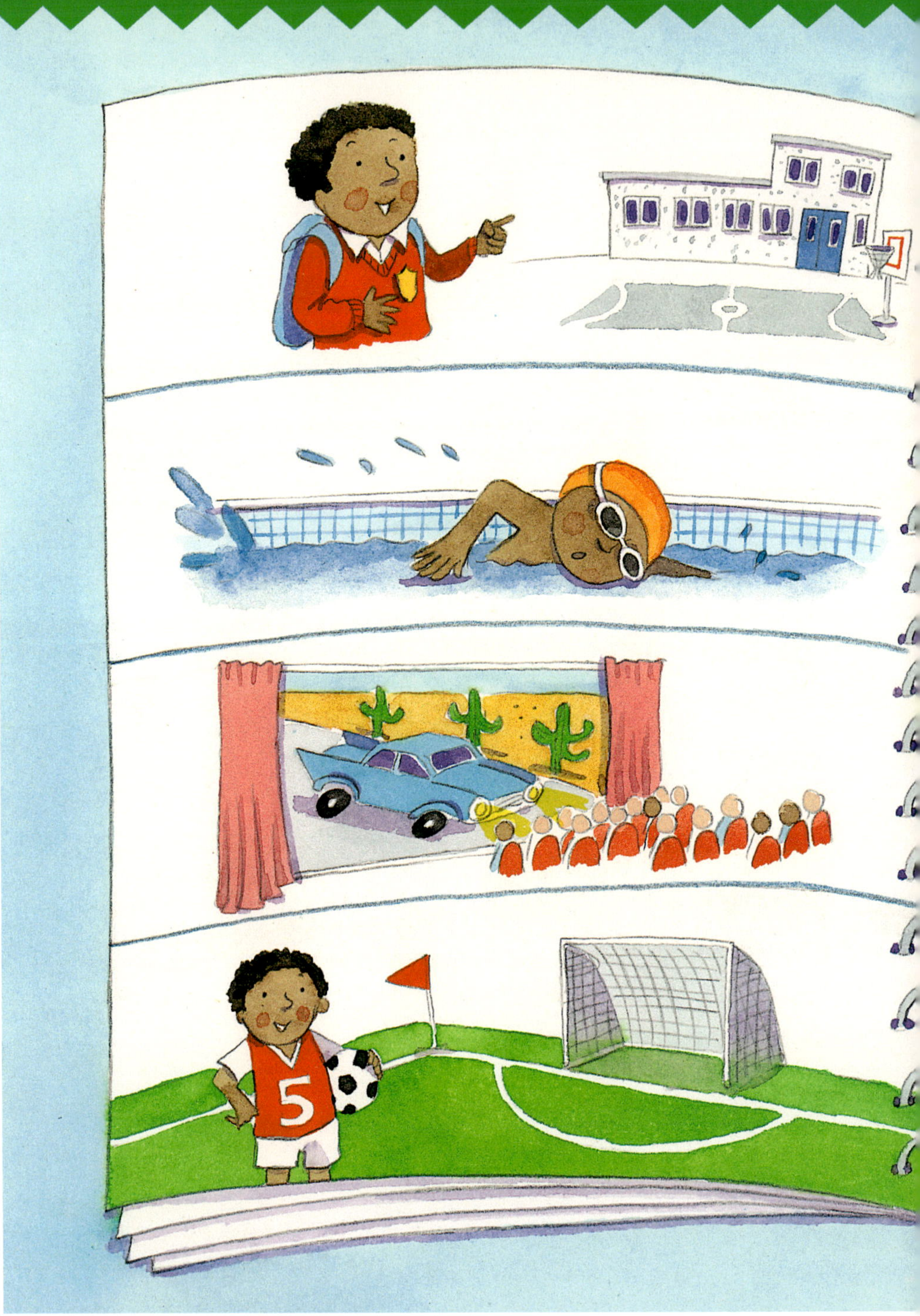

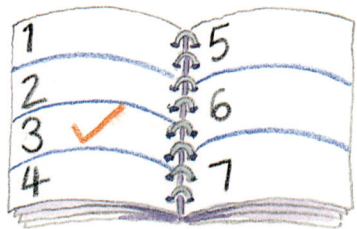

Dydd Mercher

deeth mare-kehr

Wednesday

1
2
3
4
4
5
6

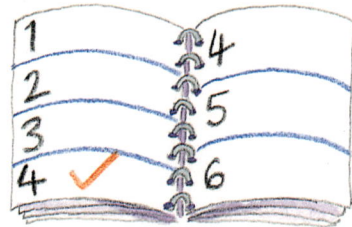

Dydd Iau

deeth ee-eye

Thursday

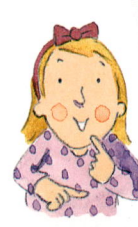

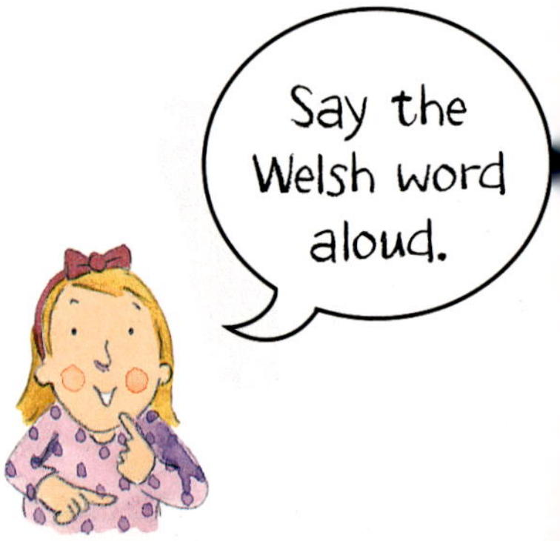

Say the Welsh word aloud.

During the week

Dydd Sul
deeth seal
Sunday

yfory
uh-voh-ree
tomorrow

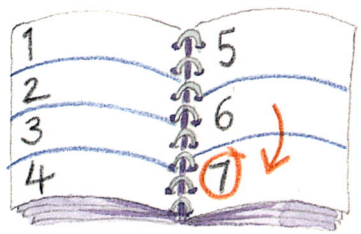

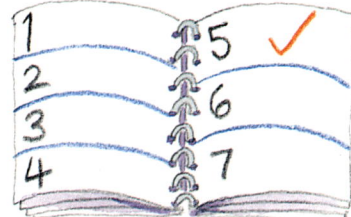

Dydd Gwener
deeth goo-ehn-her
Friday

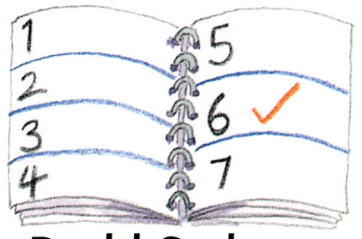

Dydd Sadwrn
deeth sad-oorn
Saturday

heddiw
heh-thew
today

Ymweld â ffrind

helô
hello
hello

na
nah
no

ie
ee-yeh
yes

plis
please
please

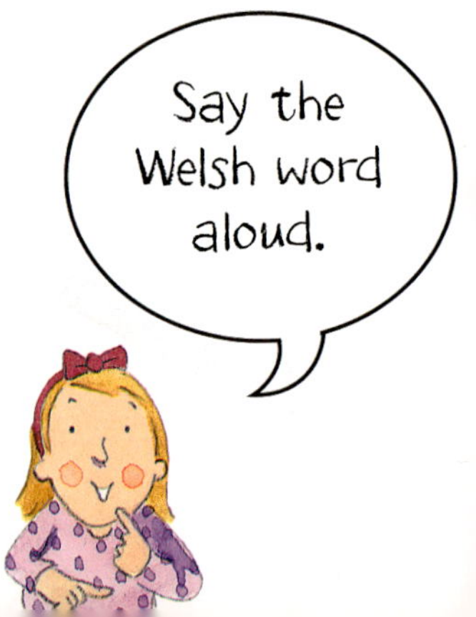

36

Visiting a friend

popeth yn iawn
pop-ehth un ee-oun
that's OK

hwyl fawr
hooeyl vour
goodbye

diolch
dee-ohlch
thank you

dyma ti
duh-ma tee
here you are

sorri
sorry
sorry

Yn y parc

Look for these words in the big picture.

merch
* merch
girl

siglen
* sea-glen
swing

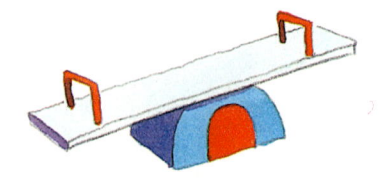

si-so
see-saw
see-saw

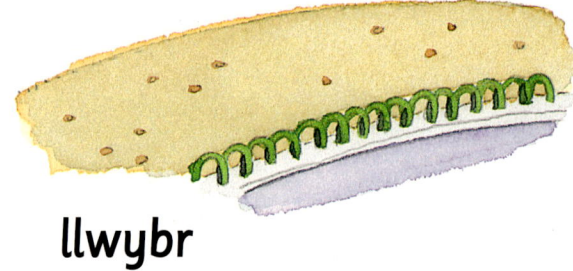

llwybr
llchoow-ee-buhr
path

Can you find a swan on another page?

At the park

bachgen
bahch-gehn
boy

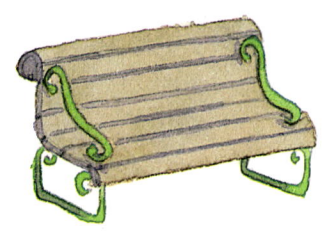

mainc
* mine-ck
bench

barcud
bahr-keet
kite

plentyn
plehn-tin
child

llyn
llch-een
lake

Say the Welsh word aloud.

Chwaraeon

Look for these words in the big picture.

tenis bwrdd
tennis boowrth
table tennis

sgio
ski-oh
skiing

pysgota
pus-got-ah
fishing

pêl-droed
pehl-droid
football

Find other sports being played in the book.

Playing sports

athletau
ahth-<u>let</u>-eye
athletics

seiclo
sye-cloh
cycling

nofio
<u>noh</u>-vee-oh
swimming

gymnasteg
* gym-<u>nahst</u>-egg
gymnastics

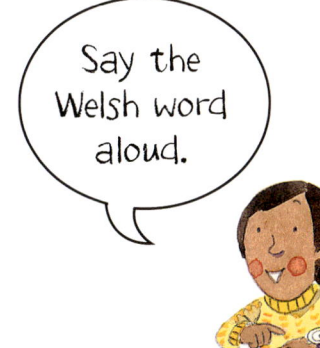

Say the Welsh word aloud.

pêl-fasged
* pehl-<u>vahs</u>-gehd
basketball

41

Yn y dref

Look for these words in the big picture.

tŷ
tee
house

gorsaf
* gohr-sahv
station

ysgol
* uhs-col
school

Find a picture that shows inside a school.

archfarchnad
* arch-varch-nad
supermarket

In town

marchnad
* <u>mahrch</u>-nad
market

siop
* shop
shop

sinema
* cinema
cinema

ffatri
* <u>fat</u>-ree
factory

swyddfa'r post
* <u>sooweeth</u>-vah'r pohst
post office

Say the Welsh word aloud.

Yn yr archfarchnad

Look for these words in the big picture.

wy
oi-ee
egg

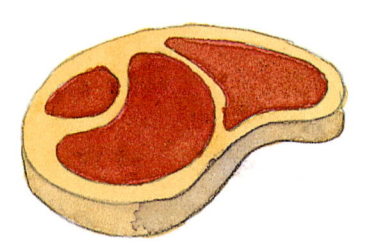

cig
kig
meat

bara
bah-ra
bread

menyn
meh-nin
butter

Find milk on another page in the book.

At the supermarket

reis
ray-ss
rice

llaeth / llefrith
llchah-eith / llche-vreeth
milk

siwgr
shoog-r
sugar

pysgodyn
pus-gohd-din
fish

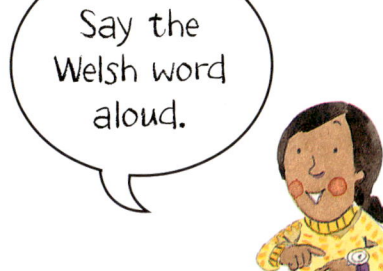

Say the Welsh word aloud.

pasta
pasta
pasta

45

Prynu ffrwythau

Look for these words in the big picture.

afal
ahv-ahl
apple

eirinen wlanog
* eheer-een-ehn oowlahn-ohg
peach

ceiriosen
* kire-eeohs-ehn
cherry

pinafal
peen-ahv-ahl
pineapple

Find some fruit in another picture.

46

Buying fruit

banana
* banana
banana

grawnwin
grahoown-ooween
grapes

mefusen
* mehv-his-ehn
strawberry

oren
* ohr-ehn
orange

mango
mango
mango

Say the Welsh word aloud.

Geiriau croes

Look for these words in the big picture.

byr
bir
short

hardd
harth
pretty

mawr
mahoor
big

drud
dreed
expensive

bach
bahkh
small

Opposites

hapus
hah-pis
happy

trist
treest
sad

da
dah
good

hir
h-eer
long

Say the Welsh word aloud.

49

Sut mae'r tywydd?

Look for these words in the big picture.

haul
haheel
sun

mae'n boeth
mine boheeth
it's hot

mae'n glawio
mine glohoow-ee-oh
it's raining

Find some rain in another picture.

cwmwl
coowm-oowl
cloud

What's the weather like?

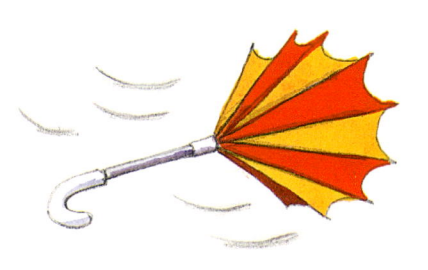

gwynt
gooweent
wind

mae'n oer
mine oi-eer
it's cold

mae'n pluo eira
mine plea-oh eyer-ah
it's snowing

storm
* stohrm
storm

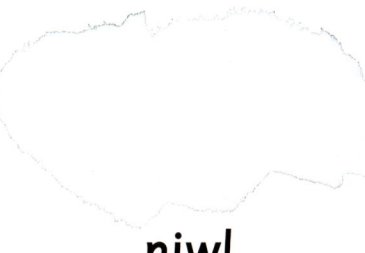

niwl
nee-oowl
fog

Say the Welsh word aloud.

Y flwyddyn – y gwanwyn a'r haf

Look for these words in the big picture.

Mawrth
mahoorth
March

Ebrill
ehbr-ellch
April

Mai
mahee
May

tymor
tuh-moor
season

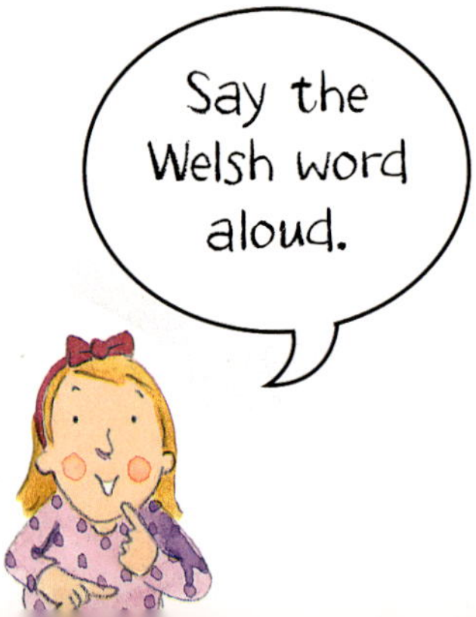

Say the Welsh word aloud.

52

The year – spring and summer

Mehefin
meh-<u>hehv</u>-een
June

Gorffennaf
gohrf-<u>ehnn</u>-ahv
July

Awst
ahoost
August

y gwanwyn
uh <u>gooahn</u>-ooeen
spring

yr haf
uhr hahv
summer

These months are autumn and winter in the Southern Hemisphere!

Y flwyddyn – yr hydref a'r gaeaf

Look for these words in the big picture.

Medi
meh-dee
September

Hydref
huhd-rev
October

Tachwedd
tahkh-ooeth
November

yr hydref
uhr huhd-rev
autumn

Say the Welsh word aloud.

The year – autumn and winter

Rhagfyr
rhahg-veer
December

Ionawr
iohn-ahoor
January

Chwefror
khooehv-rohr
February

y gaeaf
uh gay-ehv
winter

mis
mees
month

These months are spring and summer in the Southern Hemisphere!

55

Tyfu llysiau

Look for these words in the big picture.

taten
* tah-ten
potato

corn melys
kohrn meh-lees
corn

bresychen
* brehs-uhch-ehn
cabbage

moronen
*mohr-ohn-ehn
carrot

Say the Welsh word aloud.

56

Growing vegetables

tomato
tomato
tomato

letysen
* let-ees-ehn
lettuce

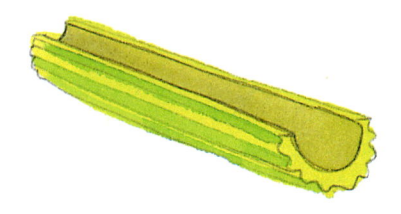

seleri
celery
celery

corbwmpen
*cohr-boowmp-ehn
courgette

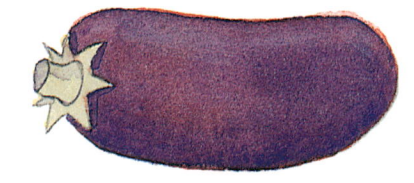

planhigyn wy
plan-heeg-in oi
aubergine

Find vegetables in another picture in the book.

57

Yn y goedwig

Look for these words in the big picture.

gwiwer
* gwee-wehr
squirrel

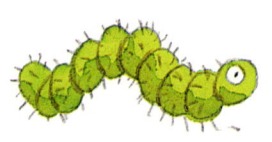

lindysyn
leend-us-in
caterpillar

carw
car-oow
deer

chwilen
* chooweel-ehn
beetle

Find a butterfly in another picture.

In the forest

arth frown
* ahrth-vrohoown
brown bear

cwningen
* coown-<u>eeng</u>-ehn
rabbit

pilipala
pee-lee-pah-la
butterfly

cadno / llwynog
<u>cad</u>-no / <u>llchwwo</u>-<u>oin</u>-ohg
fox

pryfyn
<u>pruhv</u>-in
fly

Say the Welsh word aloud.

59

Cwestiynau

Look for these words in the big picture.

pwy
p-oi-ee
who?

beth?
behth
when?

pryd?
preed?
where?

ble?
bleh?
where?

Can you think of another question?

Questions

faint?
vaent
how much?

sawl?
s-owl
how many?

ga i?
gah-ee?
can I?

pam?
pahm?
why?

sut?
sit?
how?

Say the Welsh word aloud.

Rhestr eiriau

tudalen / page 2
Ar y fferm — **On the farm**

buwch	cow
cath	cat
ceffyl	horse
ci	dog
dafad	sheep
gafr	goat
hwyaden	duck
llygoden	mouse
mochyn	pig

tudalen / page 4
Yn y dosbarth — **In the classroom**

athro	teacher
bwrdd	table
cadair	chair
cyfrifiadur	computer
glud	glue
llyfr	book
papur	paper
pen	pen
pensil lliw	coloured pencil

tudalen / page 6
Dy gorff — **Your body**

braich	arm
ceg	mouth
coes	leg
llaw	hand
llygaid	eyes
pen	head
troed	foot
trwyn	nose
ysgwyddau	shoulders

tudalen / page 8
Lliwiau yn y jyngl — **Colours in the jungle**

brown	brown
coch	red
du	black
glas	blue
gwyn	white
gwyrdd	green
melyn	yellow
oren	orange
porffor	purple

tudalen / page 10
Y bocs gwisgoedd ffansi — **The dressing-up box**

cot	coat
crys	shirt
esgidiau	shoes
ffrog	dress
het	hat
pyjamas	pyjamas
sanau	socks
sgert	skirt
trowsus	trousers

tudalen / page 12
Yn y sw p. 12 — **At the zoo**

arth wen	polar bear
crocodeil	crocodile
dolffin	dolphin
eliffant	elephant
jiráff	giraffe
hipo	hippopotamus
llew	lion
neidr	snake
teigr	tiger

tudalen / page 14
Pethau sy'n symud — **Things that go**

arhosfan bws	bus stop
bws	bus
beic	bicycle
car	car
car heddlu	police car
goleuadau traffig	traffic lights
lorri	lorry
palmant	pavement
stryd	street

tudalen / page 16
Ar y traeth — **At the beach**

cragen	shell
craig	rock
cwch hwylio	sailing boat
gwylan	seagull
gwymon	seaweed
môr	sea
pysgodyn	fish
ton	wave
tywod	sand

tudalen / page 18
Fy nheulu — **My family**

brawd	brother
cefndryd	cousins
chwaer	sister
ewythr	uncle
mam	mother
mam-gu / nain	grandmother
modryb	aunt
tad	father
tad-cu / taid	grandfather

tudalen / page 20
Amser parti! — **Party time!**

brechdan	sandwich
cacen / teisen	cake
diod swigod	fizzy drink
dŵr	water
hufen iâ	ice cream
pitsa	pitsa
sglodion	chips
siocled	chocolate
sudd oren	orange juice

tudalen / page 22
Siopa am deganau — **Shopping for toys**

cit awyren fodel	model aerokit
gêm	game
gêm gyfrifiadur	computer game
gleiniau	beads
jig-so	puzzle
pêl	ball
pêl-droed bwrdd	table football
robot	robot
tedi	teddy

tudalen / page 24
Yn y gegin — **In the kitchen**

cyllell	knife
fforc	fork
gwydr	glass
llwy	spoon
oergell	fridge
plat	plate
popty	cooker
sinc	sink
sosban	saucepan

tudalen / page 26
Yng nghefn gwlad — **In the countryside**

aderyn	bird
afon	river
blodyn	flower
cae	field
coeden	tree
coedwig	forest
mynydd	mountain
pont	bridge
porfa	grass

tudalen / page 28
Cael bath — **Having a bath**

basn ymolchi	washbasin
bath	bath
brwsh dannedd	toothbrush
cawod	shower
drych	mirror
past dannedd	toothpaste
sebon	soap
tŷ bach	toilet
tywel	towel

tudalen / page 30
Yn fy ystafell wely — **In my bedroom**

cloc larwm	alarm clock
cwpwrdd dillad	wardrobe
drws	door
ffenest	window
gwely	bed
ryg	rug
silff	shelf
sliperi	slippers
teledu	television

Word list

tudalen / page 32
Fy nhŷ — **My house**

gardd	garden
y gegin	kitchen
grisiau	stairs
lolfa	sitting room
nenfwd	ceiling
to	roof
toiled	toilet
ystafell wely	bedroom
ystafell ymolchi	bathroom

tudalen / page 34
Yn ystod yr wythnos — **During the week**

Dydd Llun	Monday
Dydd Mawrth	Tuesday
Dydd Mercher	Wednesday
Dydd Iau	Thursday
Dydd Gwener	Friday
Dydd Sadwrn	Saturday
Dydd Sul	Sunday
heddiw	today
yfory	tomorrow

tudalen / page 36
Ymweld â ffrind — **Visiting a friend**

diolch	thanks
dyma ti	here you are
helo	hello
hwyl fawr	goodbye
ie yes	yes
na	no
plis	please
popeth yn iawn	that's OK
sorri	sorry

tudalen / page 38
Yn y parc — **At the park**

bachgen	boy
barcud	kite
llwybr	path
llyn	lake
mainc	bench
merch	girl
plentyn	child
siglen	swing
si-so	see-saw

tudalen / page 40
Chwaraeon — **Playing sports**

athletau	athletics
gymnasteg	gymnastics
nofio	swimming
pêl-droed	football
pêl-fasged	basketball
pysgota	fishing
seiclo	cycling
sgïo	skiing
tenis bwrdd	table tennis

tudalen / page 42
Yn y dref — **In town**

archfarchnad	supermarket
gorsaf	station
ffatri	factory
marchnad	market
sinema	cinema
siop	shop
swyddfa'r post	post office
tŷ	house
ysgol	school

tudalen / page 44
Yn yr archfarchnad — **At the supermarket**

bara	bread
cig	meat
llaeth / llefrith	milk
menyn	butter
pasta	pasta
pysgodyn	fish
reis	rice
siwgr	sugar
wy	egg

tudalen / page 46
Prynu ffrwythau — **Buying fruit**

afal	apple
banana	banana
ceiriosen	cherry
eirinen wlanog	peach
grawnwin	grapes
mango	mango
mefusen	strawberry
oren	orange
pinafal	pineapple

tudalen / page 48
Geiriau croes — **Opposites**

bach	small
byr	short
da	good
drud	expensive
hapus	happy
hardd	pretty
hir	long
mawr	big
trist	sad

tudalen / page 50
Sut mae'r tywydd? — **What's the weather like?**

cwmwl	cloud
gwynt	wind
haul	sun
mae'n boeth	it's hot
mae'n glawio	it's raining
mae'n oer	it's cold
mae'n pluo eira	it's snowing
niwl	fog
storm	storm

tudalen / page 52
Y flwyddyn – y Gwanwyn a'r haf — **The year – Spring and summer**

Mawrth	March
Ebrill	April
Mai	May
Mehefin	June
Gorffennaf	July
Awst	August
y gwanwyn	spring
haf	summer
tymor	season

tudalen / page 54
Y flwyddyn – yr hydref a'r gaeaf — **The year – autumn and winter**

Medi	September
Hydref	October
Tachwedd	November
Rhagfyr	December
Ionawr	January
Chwefror	February
yr hydref	autumn
y gaeaf	winter
mis	month

tudalen / page 56
Tyfu llysiau — **Growing vegetables**

bresychen	cabbage
corbwmpen	courgette
corn melys	corn
letysen	lettuce
moronen	carrot
planhigyn wy	aubergine
seleri	celery
tomato	tomato
taten	potato

tudalen / page 58
Yn y goedwig — **In the forest**

arth frown	brown bear
cadno / llwynog	fox
carw	deer
cwningen	rabbit
chwilen	beetle
gwiwer	squirrel
lindysyn	caterpillar
pilipala	butterfly
pryfyn	fly

tudalen / page 60
Cwestiynau — **Questions**

beth?	what?
ble?	where?
faint	how much
ga i?	can I?
pam?	why?
pryd?	when?
pwy?	who?
sawl	many
sut?	how?

63

Cyfarwyddiadau – Instructions

Dwed y geiriau'n uchel.
Say the words aloud.

Chwilia am lysieuyn mewn llun arall yn y llyfr.
Find vegetables in another picture in the book.

Edrycha am y geiriau yma yn y llun mawr.
Look for these words in the big picture.

A weli di gath arall rywle yn y llyfr?
Can you find another cat somewhere in the book?

A weli di gadair arall rywle yn y llyfr?
Can you find another chair somewhere in the book?

Cyfra faint o blant sydd yn y parti.
Count the number of children at the party.

Faint o bethau porffor sydd yn yr olygfa?
How many purple things are in the scene?

Chwilia am rywun ar dudalen arall sy'n gwisgo het.
Find someone on another page wearing a hat.

Chwilia am anifail arall yn y llyfr a allai fod yn y sw.
Find another animal in the book that could be in the zoo.

Chwilia am gar yn rhywle arall yn y llyfr.
Find a car somewhere else in the book.

Chwilia am bysgodyn ar dudalen arall.
Find a fish on another page.

Faint o bobl sy'n dy deulu di?
How many people are in your family?

Chwilia am falŵns mewn golygfa arall.
Find some balloons in another scene.

Chwilia am dedi mewn golygfa arall.
Find a teddy bear in another scene.

Chwilia am wydryn ar dudalen arall.
Find a glass on another page.

Chwilia am aderyn arall yn y llyfr.
Find another bird in the book.

Chwilia am ystafell ymolchi ar dudalen arall yn y llyfr.
Find a bathroom on another page in the book.

Chwilia am wely mewn llun arall yn y llyfr.
Find a bed in another picture in the book.

Chwilia am dŷ arall yn y llyfr.
Find another house in the book.

Beth wyt ti'n ei wneud heddiw?
What are you doing today?

A weli di alarch ar dudalen arall?
Can you find a swan on another page?

Chwilia am gampau eraill sy'n cael eu chwarae yn y llyfr hwn.
Find other sports being played in this book.

Chwilia am lun sy'n dangos tu mewn yr ysgol.
Find a picture that shows inside a school.

Chwilia am laeth ar dudalen arall yn y llyfr.
Find milk on another page in the book.

Chwilia am ffrwyth arall mewn llun arall.
Find another fruit in another picture.

Chwilia am y glaw mewn llun arall.
Find the rain in another picture.

Mae'r misoedd hyn yn hydref ac yn aeaf yn Hemisffer y De!
These months are autumn and winter in the Southern Hemisphere!

Mae'r misoedd hyn yn wanwyn ac yn haf yn Hemisffer y De!
These months are spring and summer in the Southern Hemisphere!

Chwilia am lysiau mewn llun arall yn y llyfr.
Find vegetables in another picture in the book

Chwilia am bilipala mewn llun arall.
Find a butterfly in another picture.

Alli di feddwl am gwestiwn arall?
Can you think of another question?

Atebion – Answers

Tudalen / Page 2
Mae cath arall ar dudalennau 24, 29 a 44.

Tudalen / Page 4
Mae cadeiriau eraill ar dudalennau 18, 19, 25, 31 a 32.

Tudalen / Page 6
Mae yna 12 o blant yn y parti.

Tudalen / Page 8
Mae tri pheth porffor yn yr olygfa.

Tudalen / Page 10
Mae rhywun yn gwisgo het ar dudalennau 8, 16, 20, 40, 44, 48, 51, 53, 55, 56, 60 a 61.

Tudalen / Page 12
Mae yna anifeiliaid eraill a allai fod yn y sw ar dudalennau 8, 55 a 58.

Tudalen / Page 14
Mae car ar dudalen 34.

Tudalen / Page 16
Mae pysgod ar dudalennau 45 a 46.

Tudalen / Page 20
Mae balwnau ar dudalennau 6 a 7.

Tudalen / Page 22
Mae tedi ar dudalen 30 ac ar dudalen 33.

Tudalen / Page 24
Mae gwydrynnau ar dudalennau 18, 20, 21, 36 a 37.

Tudalen / Page 26
Mae adar ar dudalennau 2, 8, 16, 17, 26, 32, 39, 46 a 52.

Tudalen / Page 28
Mae ystafell ymolchi ar dudalen 32.

Tudalen / Page 30
Mae gwely ar dudalen 32.

Tudalen / Page 32
Mae tai ar dudalennau 2 a 35.

Tudalen / Page 38
Mae alarch ar dudalen 27.

Tudalen / Page 40
Mae campau eraill i'w gweld ar dudalennau 34 a 50.

Tudalen / Page 42
Mae llun yn dangos tu mewn yr ysgol ar dudalennau 4 a 5.

Tudalen / Page 44
Mae llaeth ar dudalen 24.

Tudalen / Page 46
Mae ffrwyth ar dudalennau 15, 18 a 24.

Tudalen / Page 50
Mae glaw ar dudalennau 52 a 53.

Tudalen / Page 56
Mae llysiau ar dudalennau 18, 21 a 35.

Tudalen / Page 58
Mae pilipala ar dudalennau 8, 9 a 26.